DISCOVER

The Sidewalks of New York City

DISCOVER

The Sidewalks of New York City

BY LOUISE QUAYLE

PHOTOGRAPHY BY JOE VIESTI

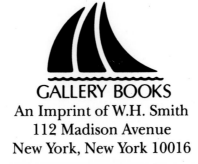

GALLERY BOOKS
An Imprint of W.H. Smith
112 Madison Avenue
New York, New York 10016

A FRIEDMAN GROUP BOOK

Published by GALLERY BOOKS
An imprint of W. H. Smith Publishers, Inc.
112 Madison Avenue
New York, New York 10016

ISBN 0-8317-6368-X

DISCOVER THE SIDEWALKS OF NEW YORK CITY
was prepared and produced by
Michael Friedman Publishing Group, Inc.
15 West 26th Street
New York, New York 10010

Editor: James K. Blum
Art Director: Robert W. Kosturko
Photo Editor: Christopher C. Bain
Production Manager: Karen L. Greenberg

All photographs © Viesti Associates.
Viesti Associates is a stock-photography library
with offices in New York City and Austin, Texas.

Color separations by Hong Kong Scanner Craft Company, Ltd.
Printed and bound in Hong Kong by Leefung-Asco Printers, Ltd.

CONTENTS

Introduction

Capturing the world's attention in fashion and the arts, and leading it in commerce and finance, New York is the capital of everything—and nothing. When people around the world imagine the land of opportunity, they usually envision New York. Even New Yorkers are sometimes guilty of seeing Manhattan as an island larger than the rest of the country. New York offers more opportunities for more people than nearly any other city in the world. It sweeps up visitors and inhabitants alike in its legendary energy, rich and varied history, electrifying pace, and endless possibility for adventure. Time and again, New York proves itself the undisputed capital of the world's metropolises.

New York's diversity is not easily described. How can one define its essence when its seven to eight million inhabitants (and millions of visitors) will give you as many answers? While many argue that its myriad personalities are shaped by its people, others insist that this multiplicity is shaped, ironically, by New York's physical limitations. Where else but in a city whose center is a tiny sixteen-mile island can such ranges of wealth, architecture, and culture be found on one city block?

At work or at play, the inhabitants ultimately do create the city's character, but its physical presence—squared-off streets, angular buildings, concrete texture, park oases, and breath-taking skyline—sets the pace for New Yorkers. For better or worse, New Yorkers have developed unique ways to live, work, and play. This is a tribute to the spatial geometry that shapes New York's self-image and to the creativity and eccentricity that drive its inhabitants. Even a city that never sleeps pauses once in a while to let a passerby muse on its wonders.

PART ONE

New York Growing

Manhattan's ideal location for trade and its three layers of solid rock—Manhattan schist, Inwood marble, Fordham gneiss—allowed it to develop up and up (previous page). Governor Peter Minuit bought the island of Manhattan for just a few trinkets in 1621—five years after the Dutch West India Company settled the colony of New Amsterdam. The lush, tree-lined Battery Park in lower Manhattan is still home to the Dutch fort where a relief commemorating the event is located (previous page inset).

No city in the world juxtaposes the modern skyscraper and the old residence as gracefully as New York. Developing from Battery Park, the home of Old New York, to Midtown and the Upper East and West sides, the city tells the story of incredible growth and change. The progression from New York's nineteenth-century brownstones to its square, white-brick apartment buildings can be seen in just one city block. The different personalities of its many neighborhoods spring from this diverse architecture, as well as from the economic realities and rich cultural heritage of New York's inhabitants.

New York's famous skyline tells the story not only of architectural tastes, but also of the city's ever-changing population and industry. As New York's economy boomed during the early 1900s, so did its physical plan, looking ever upward, striving to be the best and the most breathtaking. Built ingeniously on a grid to withstand the influx of millions of resi-

*T*o conserve space on this tiny island, New York's buildings have had to reach skyward. The tallest building in 1902, the Flatiron Building offers a striking contrast to the squared-off skyscrapers of most city blocks; it maintains its architectural integrity while making the best use of the awkward space where Broadway intersects Fifth Avenue and Twenty–third Street.

dents, the system's practicality worked with New Yorkers' aesthetic sense and need to incorporate human elements. New York is dotted with parks—including Central Park, that is at once a playground and a tribute to nature. Even skyscrapers, once intimidating to pedestrians, evolved; their open atria now welcome visitors, and their profile has softened against a horizon interspersed with lush green. From the ornate architectural styles of the nineteenth and early twentieth centuries to the dawn of modernism, New York's structures both document the history of several generations of New Yorkers and set the pace by which they live.

*A*s the skyscraper grew taller, the materials that facilitated its construction—steel and glass—inspired sparse, stripped-down facades. The modern approach, reflected in these square exteriors, eliminated the extraordinary ornamentation that characterized early twentieth century designs.

*M*anhattan adopted its famous grid system in 1811 to offer maximum space for buildings, pedestrians, and traffic. Though New York normally races at a frenetic pace, even this powerful city bows to a raging January snowstorm. The Metropolitan Life Tower (inset, foreground), another building competing to be the tallest, was built in 1909 during the economic boom of the early twentieth century. An unplanned city, New York has developed its own sense of architectural continuity, balancing the monolithic buildings of business with the living needs of its people. Here, the Con Edison clocktower (inset, background) and the residential Zeckendorf Towers, completed in 1987, echo the Metropolitan Tower's grandeur.

*T*he row houses and brownstones of the nineteenth century offered affordable, single-family dwellings. Yet rising prices and New York's increasing population of low-income families led to the development of six-story tenements in the early twentieth century. Today the city's dwellings are renter-dominated, but at the time, middle- and upper-class New Yorkers were reluctant to give up their homes for apartments. The reputations of the first multiple-family dwellings were less than desirable.

*T*he Beaux Arts-style Ansonia Hotel on the Upper West Side was built—in

the tradition of the luxurious Dakota—to lure "respectable" New Yorkers to apart-

ment living during the late nineteenth and early twentieth centuries.

W

all Street and Broadway, the site of Trinity Church, was once the northern border of old New York. Today, it is a symbol of the city's fascinating past as well as the heart of the world's most powerful financial center. While many visitors think of cosmopolitan Fifth Avenue as typical New York, others know of wonderful establishments that are off the beaten path. New York can't boast one tavern for every twelve men as it did in 1647, but McSorley's Old Ale House (above), one of the oldest bars in the city, is still one of the best places for a frosty mug of Irish brew.

*U*ptown or downtown, when snow blankets the city its inhabitants pause to bask in the city's special winter glow (opposite page). Thousands of people crowd the streets surrounding Rockefeller Center in December to watch the lighting of the Christmas tree. Looking down at the huge tree through the Channel Garden, the angels may well be trumpeting John D. Rockefeller's famous motto (a la Thomas Jefferson): "I believe in the supreme work of the individual and in his right to life, liberty, and the pursuit of happiness.

*F*ounded in 1870, the Metropolitan Museum of Art (top) was instrumental in turning the mercantile New York of the early nineteenth century into a world cultural center. The main hall is a testament to the vast collection of art housed there. Andrew Carnegie, among other wealthy New Yorkers, helped make their city a cultural mecca. The Cooper-Hewitt Museum (bottom), the Smithsonian Institution's National Museum of Design, houses its collection in his former residence. The building itself is as magnificent a tribute to design as is the museum's collection, which ranges from hair dryers to tableware.

*S*tarting at the top of this helix, visitors view the Guggenheim Museum's collection of modern art. The building, designed by Frank Lloyd Wright, startled New Yorkers; they had come to expect the modern city's skyline to keep pushing squarely upward.

*T*he harbor (below) shapes New York's "island unto itself" demeanor. The Queen Elizabeth II leaves the pier with the grandeur and elegance many people equate with New York. A symbol of freedom and liberty, and, for some, the essence of New York, is the Statue of Liberty (opposite page left). Her new facade was cheered enthusiastically by millions of New Yorkers in 1986—her one-hundredth birthday. Grant's Tomb (opposite page right), overlooking the Hudson from Riverside Park, pays tribute to the legendary Civil War general who served two terms as President. Though Ulysses S. Grant lived in New York City for only four years (1881-1885), his resting place on the Hudson is appropriate since he began his career at West Point, just a few miles up the river. Dedicated in 1897 and named a national memorial in 1959, the memorial's gray granite, classically inspired exterior and white marble interior house the sarcophagi of Grant and his wife, Julia Dent Grant.

*C*rystal-clear skylines of New York dominate the outsider's image of the city (previous page). However, on a hot summer day, the haze threatening to cloud the tops of its famous buildings lends the city a mysterious air. The Brooklyn Bridge's Gothic arches reach gracefully skyward, reflecting the optimism of its fin-de-siecle designers, while the towers of the World Trade Center, the ultimate modern skyscrapers, boldly stretch above the rest of the city (left) .

Enterprise

Although for the first few years it was only a small fur-trading port, by 1775 New York had grown to be the colonies' major metropolis; from 1820 to 1960 it was the world's largest and busiest port. Its initial development as a center for trade and commerce attracted rich and poor, the businessperson and artist, infusing New York with unparalleled cultural and ethnic diversity.

To New Yorkers, "work" can mean trading on Wall Street or painting portraits for passersby. The New Yorker's unending and uncanny ability to make work unusual, creative, entrepreneurial, and often fun remains unsurpassed. To be sure, there's money to be made here, but for many New Yorkers work is as much play as it is business. The competitive spirit of the lively streets brings out the creativity in everyone—from the one-man band or sidewalk muralist to the Madison-Avenue advertising executive or East Village publisher. With so many diverse cultures to form its work ethic, it's no wonder that the day-to-day business of New York can sometimes seem like play.

New York's roots are in lower Manhattan (previous page) where the Dutch West India Company merchants first loaded ships with beaver, otter, and mink skins. Today's industries in the downtown area are service- and finance-oriented. Even in an age of telecommunications, New York City businesses rely on the bike messenger (previous page inset).

*C*hinatown's fish markets (left) are a facet of the cultural diversity of New Yorkers at work. They also recall the heyday of New York's prominence as a port during the late nineteenth and early twentieth centuries. Its bustling harbor trade paved the way for the rapid emergence of New York as a leader in the money trade. Today the New York Stock Exchange is the world's financial barometer (below).

*O*fficially a borough of New York City, Staten Island is one of the city's most homogenous sectors: a population profile might appear more suburban than urban. Thousands of Staten Islanders commute via one of the world's most scenic harbor tours, the Staten Island Ferry.

*I*nformation is given freely to Metropolitan Museum visitors (inset). The same kind of spirit that built the most powerful financial center also built an unparalleled mecca for arts and entertainment. Radio City Music Hall (right), the largest indoor theater in America, is home to the famous Rockettes.

*A*t a Fourth of July Festival, Troupe Makandal combines complex jazz
and African rhythms to produce a cross-cultural, universal sound.

*O*utside the Guggenheim Museum, the artist goes to work, expressing both his artistic vision and entrepreneurial talent.

41

*O*ver two million visitors a year attend The Bronx Zoo's hundreds of exhibits, which display some 4,000 animals. Camel rides in the Zoo's Wild Asia section are one of the most popular events.

*uch of what makes New York such fun–the Macy's Thanksgiving Day Parade (left), for example–has evolved through the hard work of many people over the years. From design and construction of the floats, to the all-night process of inflating the colorful balloons, to coordinating the participants, the smooth spectacle of the parade isn't quite as effortless as it may seem.

*rawing runners from all over the world, the prestigious New York City Marathon (above) provides spectators and participants alike a friendly outlet for their competitive spirit.

45

*A*s the song goes, New York is the city that never sleeps. (Right) Outsiders may think of New York's luxurious limousines as the elite's respite from harrowing traffic, but they are more like traveling board rooms. To keep up with the pace, executives may use their twenty-minute ride to the airport to make a few important phone calls or dash off a memo. (Below) The old adage, "time is money," certainly applies to commuters who race through Grand Central Station. Atop the information booth in the terminal's grand main hall, this clock has sped travelers on their way since the days when a train trip was nearly as luxurious as an ocean cruise.

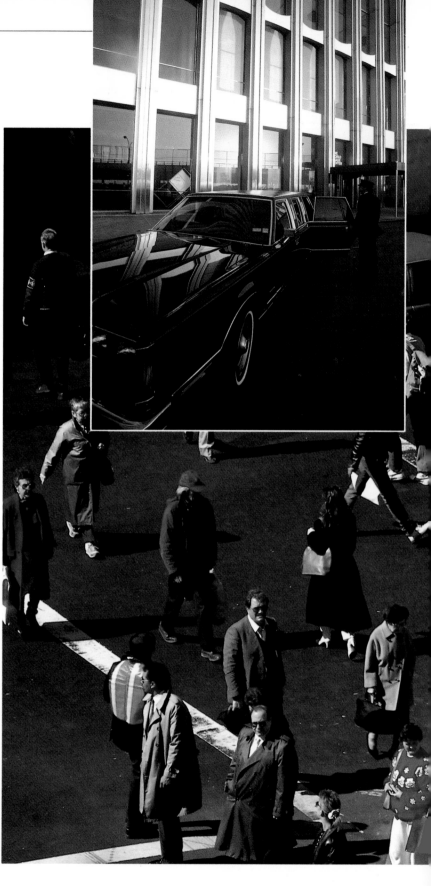

*M*idtown Manhattan, with its conglomeration of corporate headquarters for everything from clothing designers and banks to publishers and small businesses, thrives on the support of the cabs, bike messengers, and others that set the pace in the streets below.

*P*roving that fun and profit can go hand in hand, a one-man band entertains spectators at the celebration of the reopening of the Statue of Liberty on July 4, 1986.

*S*outh Street Seaport was once home to the Fulton Fish Market and a busy area for ships delivering goods from overseas. Today, South Street's Maritime Museum and complex of shops make tourism its main industry, though seafood is still the favored fare.

*M*any would argue that Milan or Paris has replaced New York as the

fashion capital of the world. A weekday walk through the garment district between

Sixth and Eighth Avenues in Midtown Manhattan tells a different story: The

streets teem with clothing racks being pushed from warehouse to vendor.

A center of intellectual prowess, New York is a haven for writers and students (right). Even though the steps of the

New York Public Library face busy Fifth Avenue, one student finds them as suitable a study retreat as the library's quiet, rich-

ly paneled reading room.

The Hansom cab, once a transportation necessity, now provides romantic visions of days gone by in Central Park and on Fifth Avenue.

Most New Yorkers rely on mass transit, though some of the colorful

cabbies make an occasional taxi ride a thrill. The cab driver's talent for conversa-

tion and storytelling is legendary, and this one would probably fill your ear with

as much as he's filled his cab.

PART THREE

Playing

*A*lice's friends in New York's wonderland take some time to enjoy Central Park (previous page inset). Lincoln Center's fountain (previous page) is at the center of a cultural wonderland that demands the best from its performers, who in turn offer the finest dance, music, and opera. A woman in Harlem engages in one of New York's favorite summertime activities–just plain sitting back and watching the people go by (right). Street performers earn their living by making work look like play. The "golden age" of street performing is said to have been during the 1970s, but plenty of artists still line the streets offering dance, music, art, and humor (inset right).

F ew cities rival the number of activities New York offers for sheer entertainment. Central Park alone, the city's outdoor leisure center, offers roller skating, cycling, Hansom-cab rides, picnics, playing fields, outdoor concerts and drama, a zoo, mini-marathons, folk dancing, magic shows, horseback riding, and more, making it a wonderland for play. And around the city, activities are offered by and for the varied populations that make up New York. Where else can you stop every few blocks to watch street performers, choose from hundreds of musical and dramatic venues, or simply take a break from the mid-

*P*ublic spaces such as this atrium testify to the New Yorker's gift for mixing work with play, offering respite from Midtown's hectic work day.

town pace in one of many "public spaces?" Even Alice in Wonderland would be delighted and amazed at what's here.

New York's first settlers had a reputation for irreverence that incited the wrath of the puritanical Governor Stuyvesant. Today, New York's residents and officials celebrate their ancestors' verve. The city's inhabitants, from the image- and art-obsessed East Villagers to the heterogenous Upper East Siders to the Chinese, Italians, Vietnamese, and more, define "play" in many different ways: it could mean anything from a relaxing summer day in the park to the bizarre and colorful displays at the Easter parade to the epitome of dramatic and musical sophistication at Lincoln Center. Anything can happen in Wonderland: New Yorkers and visitors alike revel in its many surprises and enchanting personalities.

*D*owntown, after the Fulton Market lost its prominence, the South Street Seaport area was a quiet and isolated neighborhood full of original nineteenth-century architecture. Then developers brought in a complex of shops and restaurants that now attracts nearby Wall Streeters for a drink after work and tourists for respite from a hectic day of sightseeing.

59

*T*he mayor of New York has tried to attract cyclists
to city streets by setting up bike lanes, but skateboarders
probably won't enjoy the same privilege. They're more at
home in playgrounds, where artfully sculpted steel and
mounded cement seem tailor-made for their sport.

*O*ver 240,000 people work in the offices at Rockefeller Center. But its developer, John D. Rockefeller, also wanted to provide a place to play, so he included a skating rink, a television and radio center, and fine restaurants (previous page).

*T*he brilliant marks of muralists and graffiti artists enliven the urban landscape (right). New York's Easter Parade brings out the best in everyone (above).

Manhattan Beach, just a few minutes away by train, is really in Brooklyn, but these lunchtime sunbathers don't seem to know that.

*P*unk rockers, part of the kaleido-
scope of color and expression in the
East Village (top left), play harder
than most. In a quieter moment, this
girl engages in an activity popular
with all kinds of New Yorkers–stoop
sitting. You might expect to find a
man with this much character (above)
only in a children's book, but New
Yorkers pride themselves on their range
of slightly erratic behavior in all
aspects of life. Even the leisure activity
of sunbathing offers opportunities for
innovation.

*A*s early as 1840, New Yorkers were considering a plan for a large park to
provide a natural escape from the city's maze of streets and buildings. Ever since
Central Park was completed in the late nineteenth century, sailboat enthusiasts
have navigated miniature yachts through the waters of Conservatory Pond.

Once filled with fishing boats and trading ships from all over the world,

Manhattan's waters are now plied by pleasure boats. For a view from the water,

try the Circle Line.

*M*usic fills the city's streets in the summertime. One man moves to his own sounds through the streets of Hell's Kitchen.

Not exactly New York's version of Alice's tea party, St. Marks Place in the

East Village comes close by offering a little something (often something bizarre) for

everyone: books, politics, movies, music, theater, and, of course, eats.

*S*pringtime brings out the nature lover in New Yorkers, who flock to Central

Park for a stroll or a picnic.